The Power that's Ours

Gary Hirson

Illustrated by Carmen Ziervogel

The Power that's Ours
by Gary Hirson

Published by Calm in Storm 2009
www.calminstorm.com

Copyright © Calm in Storm 2009
PO Box 12018, Mill Street, 8010, Cape Town
1st edition, 2009
2nd edition, 2010

Print book ISBN 978-0-620-43213-9
Ebook ISBN 978-0-620-43214-6

Written by Gary Hirson
gary@garyhirson.com
Cell: 0836082194

Illustrated by Carmen Ziervogel
carmen.ziervogel@gmail.com

Set in Adobe Caslon Pro and Afrika Potyi
Designed and produced by Mousehand

ABOUT THE AUTHOR

Gary Hirson is a photographer, writer and entrepreneur with a keen interest in the magic of creativity. His first book, *The Magic that's Ours*, helps children discover and explore the realm of imagination. His second book, *The Power that's Ours*, hopes to introduce children to the concepts of goal setting, visualisation and affirmation.

ACKNOWLEDGEMENTS

Thanks to Janyce Weintrob for being such a good sounding board, editor and friend. Catherine Normand – Educational Psychologist – whose expert opinion helped guide me with the final details of the book. Robin Malan for his legal and very experienced input. Isabel Essery for her time and valued input regarding the final edit. Carmen Ziervogel for the fantastic illustrations. Electric Book Works for the amazing design work. Special thanks to Amy Falconer and Zac Abel, whose great feedback reassured me that the story and message are more than acceptable.

Special acknowledgement is made to John Kehoe and Nancy Fischer for the term "magical thinking" as used on page 31 onwards. (John Kehoe: *Mind Power for Children*, Zoetic Inc, Vancouver, Canada, 2002).

1

It had been raining the whole night and it was still dark when Joel and Jina woke up. Joel could hear the rain tapping softly against his window and he groaned as he rolled over and pulled the blankets up tighter under his chin. Winter was not Joel and Jina's favourite time of year as it was always cold and dark, and usually wet when the brother and sister had to get ready for school. Both of them tried to snuggle under the covers for as long as possible, testing their mom's patience during the school week. She had to repeatedly shout up to them to get out of bed and get ready for school.

Only when they could hear a note of real irritation in their mom's voice did they drag themselves wearily down the stairs to the breakfast table.

Joel, who was older than his sister, was already eating his breakfast this morning when Jina entered the kitchen.

They were close as a brother and sister, but like any other 10 and 11-year-old siblings they would often tease each other. He took one look at Jina and remarked, "Geez Jina, what's up with you? You look like you didn't sleep a wink!"

"Thanks Joel, I love you too," she replied sarcastically.

Joel chuckled. "So what's it then? I haven't seen you like this for a long time."

"I'm competing in the showjumping gymkhana to-morrow, and I'm really nervous about it. The weather isn't going to be great and the selectors from the national team are going to be there. I really don't want to mess up," she replied.

"Don't worry about it, sis! You're going to be fine, you always do well at these things," Joel said, with milk running down his chin.

Jina sat down and started playing with her cereal, too absorbed to eat much.

"Come on, let's go – we don't want to be late for school … again!" said Joel.

They were very lucky, because they lived just a short distance from school, and could walk there in no time at all. All they had to do was cross the road and walk through a small field. At the end of the field was a stream, which they crossed by jumping over the smooth rocks. The school yard was just a stone's throw away.

The whole walk took about ten minutes, but Joel and Jina loved being outside and always stopped to look at the birds and the plants, and to listen to the insects.

Jina liked the birds and the butterflies. She would stand transfixed, admiring their bright colours and listening to their birdsong. Joel liked the green hairy caterpillars and would often pick one up and let it crawl up his arm. He loved the tingly sensation.

When they were younger he would try to scare Jina by sneaking one of the caterpillars down her jersey. Every once in a while he would still try, but these days they would usually just talk about and marvel at the beauty of all the little creatures they saw on their walk.

But today was different. Jina was feeling really down and was thinking hard about tomorrow's gymkhana. She was thinking so much about it that she never took her eyes off the pathway and so she missed out on seeing all the colourful birds, insects and flowers. Joel let her be and they walked together in silence, when …

Everything around them began to change.

The frogs stopped croaking.

The birds stopped tweeting.

The dogs stopped barking.

The stream continued to flow over the boulders, but made no sound.

The rustle of the breeze through the trees stopped, and even Joel and Jina's breathing couldn't be heard.

As the silence fell, the colours of the grass, the sky, the stream, the plants and insects became much brighter. They weren't frightened because they had experienced this before, the first time they had met Imagi-Nashun, or Magic.

Joel and Jina looked downstream, knowing what was about to happen. The little stream usually ran down into a bed of tall reeds, but as had happened so often, they now saw what looked like the entrance to a cave. They knew that it was not a cave but rather the entrance to a big black hole, with bright colours dancing around inside. Jina's mood began to lighten, as she knew she was going to meet up with Magic once again. And she truly loved these meetings, which were always fun-filled, colourful and exciting adventures.

They raced through the entrance to the hole, stopping dead in their tracks once inside. They knew what was in store and wanted to take their time to absorb their surroundings and miss nothing.

Colours were darting in different directions, back and forth, up and down, around and about. Violet, indigo, blue, green, yellow, orange and red – the children's eyes were filled with the most awesome colours imaginable – as the big black hole became a tunnel of shimmering, cascading light.

As Joel and Jina walked further into the tunnel, it felt as though they were walking on air. When they looked down at their feet, all they could see was what looked like the night sky – with millions of bright shiny stars floating beneath them. They loved this feeling and carried on further along the starry pathway, knowing it would take them to a place of absolute delight and splendour.

Joel looked at the wall of the tunnel closest to him and realised that the flashing colours were actually a giant video, a video of all the dreams he had. They weren't like the dreams he had while he was sleeping, rather, they were his dreams and goals for the future. All the things he wanted to do, to buy and to become were flashing on the wall in front of his eyes. He even saw his dream of him holding Francesca's hand as they sat under the big willow tree at school. He suddenly became embarrassed because nobody knew he liked Francesca, and that he wanted her to be his girlfriend.

He quickly turned to see if Jina had seen this, but she was too preoccupied looking at her own dreams. She was watching her fear-filled dream of herself falling from her horse in front of the judges.

Joel noticed her eyes filling with tears. He took her hand and gave it a gentle squeeze.

Joel said, "Come on Jina, let's go see Magic. He'll make it right."

Jina tried to smile, but just nodded and let Joel lead her further into the tunnel.

2

After a short distance they came to the end of the tunnel and this was always the most exciting bit for both of them. Each time they had met Magic the surroundings had been different. The first time they met him was in a beautiful cavern filled with small waterfalls, chirping birds, swinging monkeys and flashing crystals. Other times they had met in a snow-filled forest with cedar trees so high they could barely see the tops. The forest was a brilliant white from all the snow and there were roaming wolves and bears. The animals weren't there to attack them, but rather to greet them and make them feel protected.

The last time they had met, it had been in the middle of a coral garden at the bottom of a deep, turquoise ocean. The coral teemed with different shapes, sizes and colours of fish darting around them. There were

lobsters, octopuses and even a massive, slow-moving humpback whale.

This time they weren't to be disappointed either. As they took a step out of the tunnel they entered the most fantastic oasis they had ever seen, in the middle of the largest desert imaginable. The sun was setting slowly, bathing the surrounding sand dunes in a warm, coppery-bronze light. Camels shaded themselves under palm trees heavy with ripe dates and juicy berries. Colourful birds flitted from tree to tree, picking off the juiciest ones. And high above them hawks circled in unison floating on the cool breeze. A fragrance of coconut and lavender wafted towards Joel and Jina as they spied a deep, serene pool of water so still and blue that it looked liked an ink-pot.

On the far side of the pool, they saw colourful Bedouin tents with nomads sitting inside, drinking tea. They looked up at Joel and Jina and waved. Their majestic horses, dappled black, brown and white were tied alongside the tents, lapping at the pool, their muscles rippling underneath their sleek coats. Joel and Jina stood with gaping mouths taking in all the beauty and splendour.

FUN TIME!

Draw, paint or sketch what you imagine the desert scene looks like!

HAVE LOADS OF FUN!

3

Just then, Imagi-Nashun appeared.

Jina had always thought that he was the cutest little creature she had ever seen. He looked like a mixture of candyfloss and the wispy breath a person blows out on a cold winter's morning.

He would appear in front of them one moment and then disappear the next, although he would never be totally gone. He glowed white, pink and light blue and had large round eyes warm with friendliness. He had no legs to stand on, but floated just above the sand. And today, just for fun, he was wearing a turban, which made both Joel and Jina laugh.

"Hiya guys, it's really fantastic to see you again."

"Hi Magic!" they replied in unison.

Joel and Jina had first met Magic a year ago. He had popped up out of nowhere to explain to them about a gift that everybody has – the gift of imagination. This gift or magic was free for them to use at any time and by using it they could think up games to play, stories to tell or pictures to draw. He had stressed that they must only use their magic for good things and that how they treated people, animals and plants would be how they would be treated in return.

"Guys, I am so proud of you," said Magic. "Ever since our first meeting, I've really been impressed by how you've learnt to use your imaginations. Joel, I am amazed at how good you've become at drawing and painting, and Jina, the way you now solve problems by using your imagination is absolutely brilliant. But today I see something is bothering Jina. Something that she thinks is so big that she doesn't know how to deal with it?"

He looked at Jina and she slowly nodded her head, the sadness creeping back. "Don't worry Jina! Together we're going to work through it and sort it out so it will seem like nothing at all by the time we're finished with it!"

Even though he had been listening to what Magic was saying, Joel was looking at the Bedouins in their tents. He wanted to go and meet them and look at their horses.

"Go ahead Joel, go and meet the Bedouins and learn something about how they live. I am going to speak to Jina for a while and she can tell you all about it later."

Ever surprised that Magic knew what he was thinking, Joel didn't need a second invitation and was off in a flash.

Jina and Magic wandered off to sit under a palm tree. As Jina was getting comfortable, a small bird hovered above her and dropped a few dates in her lap. Unsurprised, she said "Thank you" and started nibbling on the sweet fruit.

"So Jina, this gymkhana is really bothering you, isn't it?"

Jina had gotten used to the fact that Magic always knew what she and Joel were thinking. She nodded and replied, "Magic, I'm so scared I'm going to fail! There are only two places left in the national team and I really want to be chosen. I want to do well so that Mom and Dad will be proud of me."

"Hmm, so why do you think you won't make the team?" he asked.

"I don't think I am good enough and I keep thinking I'm going to fall off my horse!" replied Jina, with a tear rolling down her cheek.

"And what do you think will happen if you don't get chosen?" asked Magic.

"My parents will feel so bad and people will laugh at me and I will feel ashamed!"

"Okay, so you're feeling really stressed about something before it has even happened?" quizzed Magic.

"What do you mean?" asked Jina, slightly confused.

"Jina," said Magic with a slight smile on his face, "you're thinking you're going to fail before you've even started! You think you know how you and other people are going to feel if you don't make the team. Can't you see that you're concentrating on the negatives and this is making you feel bad?

What if I were to show you a way to help you concentrate on the positives? Not only might you win the competition, but more importantly, you'll feel good about yourself and will be the happy Jina that I know so well."

Just as Jina was about to reply they heard a loud whooping sound coming from the far side of the water. They looked over to see Joel on a big black stallion, kicking its forelegs in the air. One of the Bedouins was standing in front of the horse, holding its reins while he laughed loudly at Joel having so much fun. Jina felt better watching her brother. She thought of Dreamchaser, the grey and white mare she was to ride at the gymkhana. Dreamchaser belonged to the stables, but Jina loved her as if she were her own.

Magic then asked, "Do you know what a *goal* is Jina?"

"It's when a football player kicks the ball into the net," she replied.

"Quite right," said Magic, "but there's also another answer. Do you remember when you were walking in the tunnel to get here and you saw all of those pictures like a giant video shining on the wall. Well, those were pictures of your goals and your dreams. A goal is something that you want to have, or to be, or to do, or to become."

"But there are a lot of things that I want to have and to be and to do and to become. How do I know which one is a goal?"

Magic smiled at Jina, impressed by her question.

"A goal becomes a goal when you decide that it is something you truly want. Once you've decided on a goal you make a decision to reach it and put steps into place to achieving it. And from my experience, reaching a goal can be one of the happiest experiences you will ever have."

"Oh I understand," replied Jina. I suppose me wanting to be prefect when I get to 7th grade is a goal?"

"Exactly!" exclaimed Magic. "That's exactly it. So do you think getting chosen for the national showjumping team is a goal then?" he enquired.

"Yes!" said Jina, "I know it's a goal because I want it with all my heart."

Magic was just about to speak when Jina said: "I don't want to fall off my horse, but I saw it happening on the tunnel wall before my eyes."

"Thinking you're not good enough and that you're going to fall has replaced your goal of being chosen for the national team. But I'm going to show you how to concentrate on being chosen for the team so that becomes your goal again. Ready?" asked Magic.

"Yes!" replied Jina.

"Good," said Magic. "Then let's begin!"

"I want you to write your goal down on a piece of paper exactly the way you imagine it."

Out of nowhere a writing pad and pencil appeared in her lap. She wrote, **I want to be chosen for the national showjumping team.**

"Good," he said. "But now I want you to write it in the present tense, as if you have already achieved the goal."

I AM in the national showjumping team, she wrote.

"Excellent!" said Magic. "That's perfect."

FUN TIME!

Using your magic, write down a goal for yourself. Make it something that you can achieve.

It can be anything you want to have, anything you want to do or anything you want to become.

Example: If you run the 100 metre sprint and you want to be chosen for the school athletics team, write it down so that it is in the present tense. "I run the 100 metre sprint for the school athletics team."

Keep it somewhere safe so we can use it later.

HAVE LOADS OF FUN!

4

"Now that you have written your goal down, it's important that it has feeling," said Magic.

"What do you mean, feeling?" quizzed Jina.

Magic answered, "Tell me about a time that you felt happiest and most excited, a time when you were having the most fun."

"Oh that's easy," replied Jina, "I was at a carnival with my friends and there was the most awesome fireworks display. There were clowns on stilts and magicians doing tricks. I was walking around just *loving* all the colours and sounds, and I was also eating a big, red toffee apple."

"So you were having a good time?" asked Magic.

"Oh yes!" replied Jina.

"And was the carnival something like this …?"

All of a sudden everything around them changed

and instead of sitting at the oasis, they were now walking in the middle of a festive carnival. There were orange, green, blue, gold and silver fireworks exploding across the sky.

Clowns on stilts, dressed in long shimmering red pants and yellow shirts, were ambling along while making animals out of long thin balloons. There were magicians doing card tricks and making flowers disappear. And there was a brightly-dressed marching band playing lively, foot-tapping music, while marching along together.

Jina first excitedly showed Magic the fireworks, and then the clowns, followed by the marching band and the magicians. She was so excited and happy to be there witnessing all the colours and sounds, that she didn't realise that she was eating a toffee apple!

After some time Magic tapped Jina on the shoulder and said, "How you're feeling now is how you should feel when writing your goal down or thinking about it. Also, imagine that this is the feeling you'll have when you reach your goal. We also have to go back to the oasis where it's much quieter so we can carry on talking," he said with his fingers in his ears.

And with that they were back at the oasis, Jina sitting under the date tree, just as if she hadn't left at all, apart from the fact that she was still eating her toffee apple.

Now tell me how you will feel when your name gets read out as part of the team."

"It will feel exciting and fantastic just like I'm feeling now!" beamed Jina.

"Good," replied Magic. "But tell me exactly how you'll feel when you get told that you are part of the national team. Tell me how your parents are going to feel and how Joel will react."

Jina closed her eyes and sat in silence. After a while she said, "I'll be standing with my family and friends and the judges will call out the names of the two riders that make the team. My name will be one of them. I'll be so happy that I'll just jump up and down screaming with joy. I will have the biggest smile on my face and my body will be tingling with excitement. My parents will be hugging me and my mom will probably be crying. My dad will be so proud of me. Joel will be very happy for me but I'm sure he won't hug me in front of everybody. I know he'll be chuffed all the same."

She opened her eyes and Magic could see them sparkling.

Magic asked, "Don't you think that the way you are feeling now is so much better than when you first arrived?"

Jina nodded, still smiling.

"And you see there wasn't much that I did. The only thing we did was to get you to focus on the positives."

Jina nodded again, as it all started to make sense.

"But we aren't finished yet, there's still a bit more to go."

FUN TIME!

Sit by yourself or in a group of friends and remember a time when you felt the happiest and most excited. Either write down where it was and how you felt at the time, or describe it to your friends. Remember how it felt when you were having so much fun.

HAVE LOADS OF FUN!

5

"Okay," said Magic, "now that you know what it will feel like when you're chosen for the national team, what do you have to do to make the team?"

"I have to finish first or second in the competition," replied Jina with her face clouding over, the fear starting to creep back.

"Okay, so first or second it is," replied Magic.

"Which one do you want?"

"I want to finish first!" replied Jina, becoming more confident.

"So, thinking of only the positives, what do you have to do if you want to finish first?"

"I have to get over five jumps, one with water, quicker than the other girls while also making the least mistakes. I also have to concentrate 100 per cent and I have to practise."

"Excellent," said Magic, "you must believe 100 per cent that you can do it. There's not much time before the show tomorrow so you won't be able to practise too much, but I'm happy you mentioned it. If you want to be good at something you *must* practise. But I know that you have."

"But before we carry on, I think we need another change of scenery," said Magic. "Have you ever been to Paris?"

In the blink of an eye both Jina and Magic were sitting on a platform at the top of the Eiffel Tower in Paris, France. Jina looked through the glass window and could see the whole of Paris spread out below her. She saw the Arc de Triomphe, the arch that Napoleon had built to commemorate his battle victories. She marvelled at the River Seine snaking its way through the enormous city. She gawked at the buildings of Montmartre, the artistic village of days gone by, perched majestically on top of a hill in the distance. The views were breath-taking and Jina had to catch her breath when looking at all below her. They were so high up that she could just see pigeons, gracefully flying far below her. She turned to speak to Magic, and when she did she noticed that he was not wearing a turban anymore. On his head sat a black beret, and he was dressed in an artist's apron which was splattered with paints of different colours. He was standing next to an easel that held up a blank canvas and in his hand was a palette with different paint colours blotched all around it. A paintbrush was tucked behind his ear. Jina giggled.

"Oh my gosh Magic, I can't believe it, we're on top of the Eiffel Tower, in Paris. I can't wait to tell Joel about this!"

Magic smiled, pleased that Jina was having so much fun.

"Shall we continue?" he asked.

Jina nodded, glancing once again out the window.

"Do you know what visualisation is? You could also think of it quite simply as **magical thinking**."

"No," replied Jina.

"You know that we all have our imaginations or magic and that we can think up anything we want to by using it?"

Jina nodded.

"Well when you use your magic, picture yourself reaching your goal while feeling the same way that you felt when you were at the carnival. That's visualising – or using your **magical thinking**. It's imagining, in the present tense, how it feels when you've already reached your goal. Do you understand?"

"I think so," said Jina, slightly confused.

"Okay, let's do a little fun exercise that will explain it even better. I want you to sit comfortably and close your eyes."

"To start this fun exercise you need to be relaxed, so just listen to what I say. Concentrate on your feet and feel them becoming very relaxed, all soft and squishy."

Magic waited a few moments before continuing.

"Feel your legs becoming totally relaxed and resting comfortably on the ground.

"Feel your stomach becoming soft and relaxed.

"Feel your chest moving in a gentle rhythm as you breathe gently in and out.

"Feel your arms loosely relaxed at your side.

"Feel your head comfortably on top of your neck. Your neck is relaxed and soft, sitting on top of your shoulders, and you are feeling completely relaxed.

"Now imagine yourself in a big, silver bubble. The bubble, with you in it, is anchored firmly to the ground and the walls of the bubble are made of a special material that only allows positive thoughts and feelings inside. All negative thoughts and feelings that try to get into the bubble bounce off the outside walls and are sent back to where they came from.

"Are you still with me?" asked Magic, noticing that Jina was looking totally relaxed.

She nodded slowly.

"Excellent," said Magic, "now we will begin with the **magical thinking**. I want you to imagine yourself sitting on top of your horse at the start of the showjumping course. Are you comfortable sitting on your horse?"

Jina sat silently for a while and then frowned. "I can't see anything, Magic. What's wrong with me?"

"Don't worry, sometimes it takes a while and a bit

of practice. Some people take to it easily and can *see* it happening, and some *feel* it happening. Just relax and use your imagination. Shall we try again?"

Jina nodded and started to relax straight away.

"I want you to imagine yourself sitting on top of your horse at the start of the showjumping course. Are you comfortable sitting on your horse?"

Now Jina nodded as she started to get the feel for it.

"Using your **magical thinking** I want you to go through the whole course as if you are riding in the competition now. I want you to see yourself clearing every jump comfortably. You feel happier and more excited with every jump you clear. You feel comfortable and confident knowing that your horse is listening to all your commands."

Magic waited for a few minutes and then said, "slowly rub your fingers together and become aware of where you are sitting."

Jina rubbed her fingers and stretched her legs.

"Open your eyes and tell me how you felt," Magic said.

"Wow Magic, that felt so cool! I could see myself sailing over the jumps and with every jump I cleared I got more excited and confident about clearing the next one."

As Jina was excitedly telling Magic about her experience, she looked at the easel and noticed that the once-blank canvas was now a painting. The painting was a picture of everything that Jina had just described. In perfect colours, there she was on her grey-and-white mare sailing over one of the jumps, clearing it comfortably. Gina's face in the painting was beaming with both excitement and confidence.

"That's it Magic, that's exactly what I saw and felt!" she exclaimed pointing at the picture. "Can we do that again, *please*?"

Magic laughed. "Of course we can – but first let's go over what we've just done. You've set yourself a goal and you've used your **magical thinking** to see and feel yourself reaching that goal?"

"Yes," nodded Jina, grinning from ear to ear.

FUN TIME!

Using the goal from fun time at the end of chapter 3, sit comfortably somewhere and do the following **fun relaxing exercise** to help you relax. Use your **magical thinking** to see and feel yourself reaching that goal now. Once you have finished the **fun relaxing exercise**, rub your fingers together until you feel comfortable enough to open your eyes.

HAVE LOADS OF FUN!

This fun relaxing exercise is very safe. Once you get used to it you will feel some, if not all, of the following:

Your body will feel light and relaxed.

Your breathing will soften.

You might feel a tingly sensation in your skin.

With your eyes closed you might see colours.

You will have a feeling of calmness and you will feel good.

Fun Relaxing Exercise

Concentrate on your feet and feel them becoming very relaxed, all soft and squishy.

Feel your legs becoming totally relaxed and resting comfortably on the ground.

Feel your stomach becoming soft and relaxed.

Feel your chest moving in a gentle rhythm as you breathe gently in and out.

Feel your arms loosely relaxed at your side.

Feel your head comfortably on top of your neck.

Your neck is relaxed and soft, sitting on top of your shoulders and you are feeling completely relaxed.

Now imagine yourself in a big, silver bubble. The bubble, with you in it, is anchored firmly to the ground and the walls of the bubble are made of a special material that only allows positive thoughts and feelings inside.

All negative thoughts and feelings that try and get into the bubble bounce off the outside walls and are sent back where they came from.

6

"Jina, you're doing so well but there is still one more thing. Do you know what an affirmation is?"

"I think so," replied Jina. "It's when you say nice things about yourself?"

Magic was so happy that Jina understood that he spun around almost knocking the painting over. They both fell over laughing.

Magic said, "Jina, you are so very wise. You're spot on. An affirmation is something positive we repeat to ourselves to make us feel better about ourselves. I also like calling it **magical talking** because it mysteriously helps us to change our moods and reach our goals. It is important to keep it simple, say it in the present tense, say it with feeling and believe it 100 per cent. Repeating it often helps even more.

So let's try that exercise again! This time repeat af-

My horse is listening to my commands
I am a good showjumper!
I am a good
I am a good rider
I am part of the national showjumping team!
I am good enough to win this competition!
My horse is listening to my commands
These jumps are easy to get

firmations to yourself that will make you feel even more confident about winning the show. Sit comfortably and either close your eyes, or keep them open, whichever feels better for you."

This time, Jina kept her eyes open.

"First, using the fun exercise, relax your body. Then, using your **magical thinking** and **magical talking**, I want you to go through all the steps just as before. I want you to repeat anything to yourself that is positive and that'll make you feel better and more confident about doing well in the show."

Jina sat silently for a while. After about a minute Magic could see that she was relaxed. She started using her **magical thinking** and after a while began to repeat to herself, "I am a good show jumper."

"My horse is listening to my commands."

"I am a good rider."

"These jumps are easy to get over."

"I am good enough to win this competition."

"I am part of the national showjumping team."

Magic looked on, smiling at Jina, proud of how far she had come.

"Now I want you to see yourself going through the end tape and see the clock with a time that is quicker than the other riders. I also want you to imagine how it feels to have made no mistakes over the jumps."

Jina sat there for a while with a wide grin on her face, like a person who had just won something.

"Slowly open your eyes," whispered Magic.

Jina opened her eyes and started babbling straight away. "Magic, that was fantastic. I saw myself sailing over all the jumps, easy as pie. I felt so comfortable on my horse, which was listening to all my commands. And when I started repeating all those positive things to myself I felt even more confident. I can't wait for tomorrow, I wish the show was today!"

She glanced over at the painting and noticed that, now, all the affirmations she had repeated were written on the canvas as well.

I am a good show jumper!

My horse is listening to my commands!

I am a good rider!

These jumps are easy to get over!

I am good enough to win this competition!

I am part of the national showjumping team!

The affirmations were written in all directions creating an interesting design and frame on the outside of the picture.

After Jina had calmed down Magic said, "Jina, what we have learnt today you can do whenever you want to. Any time of day or night – and the more often the better! The main thing to remember is that it must always be done for the good. You can't do it to try and harm someone or make them feel bad. You cannot concentrate on one of the other riders falling off their horse and getting hurt. You must rather concentrate on yourself doing well. And you can do this for anything in your life. If you are feeling down all you have to do is think and talk **magically** to yourself, repeating positive things that will help you feel better."

"Magic, what happens if I only finish third and I don't make the team?" asked Jina.

Magic was happy because this was the best question of all of those that Jina had asked.

"Jina, if you've tried your best and you still don't make the team, then that's fine because you've done all you could. You pat yourself on the back and say 'Well done'.

"Your parents will still be proud of you and they will love you just as they love you today. You won't have to feel ashamed because you tried with all your heart. What you need to do is try your hardest, have fun and enjoy every minute of what you do.

"And now we must go," said Magic.

"Can I keep the painting?" asked Jina.

"Of course," replied Magic, "and the best thing to do is to hang it somewhere where you can see it every day. Look at it daily and read the affirmations."

FUN TIME!

Find pictures in magazines or, using many colours, draw a picture that's related to your goal from chapter 3.

Example 1. If you want to swim for

your school's swimming team then find or draw pictures of swimmers.

Draw or cut the pictures out and glue them on a piece of thin board.

Under the pictures write 5 short affirmations or phrases that connect the pictures to your goal.

Example: "I am a great swimmer" or "I swim very fast ."

Put the board up somewhere where you can look at it often (like next to your bed or on a mirror).

Take time out every day to look at the pictures and imagine that it is you in the pictures.

Read the affirmations out loud every morning when you wake up and every evening before you go to bed. Remember to repeat them with feeling.

You can also repeat them to yourself any time you want.

HAVE LOADS OF FUN!

7

Back at the oasis once again, Jina looked over to see what Joel was up to. He was on the back of a stallion being led by one of the Bedouins towards her and Magic.

When Joel got back, Magic asked, "Did you have fun Joel, did you learn anything new?"

Joel was so excited he just started rambling on about all he had learnt from his new friends. Magic laughed and said, "Joel, Jina has also learnt a lot today. She'll tell you all about it now before you go off to school. As you both know, when we're together, what seems like hours to you is really just seconds. Soon you will be back in the field across from your school. But as always, you'll be late. Now I must be on my way. Until we meet again then," he said with a wave of his hand. And with that he was gone.

Joel and Jina sat under the palm tree eating dates. Joel listened to everything that Jina was telling him, but he was slightly distracted because he was thinking about the fun he had had with his new friends, the Bedouins.

Jina finished talking just as a sandstorm started brewing on the outskirts of the oasis. It grew bigger and bigger and moved closer and closer.

Just as it reached them they shut their eyes and held on to each other tightly. In an instant they were blanketed in a swirling cloak of darkness. The soft sand moved around them in all directions, gently massaging their faces, legs and arms. A few seconds later, as quickly as it had started, the sandstorm was over. They opened their eyes and saw that they were back in the field across from their school. The oasis, palm trees, lake and Bedouins were no longer there. Just then they heard the bell ring for the start of school ...

FUN TIME!

Using the goal from chapter 3, sit somewhere comfortably. With eyes open or closed, whichever feels better, do the **fun relaxing exercise**. Then practise your **magical thinking** and **talking by** imagining yourself reaching that goal. Once you have finished the **fun relaxing exercise**, rub your fingers together and stretch your legs.

HAVE LOADS OF FUN!

8

Joel and Jina arrived at school late, once again. But they were too excited to be worried about getting into trouble. They said goodbye and rushed to their classrooms.

Joel burst into the classroom, but luckily his teacher, Ms. Samaai, had been called down to the headmaster's office.

He sat down next to his friend Keilash and excitedly told him the whole story. Keilash thought he was crazy and was just about to tell him so when Ms. Samaai entered the room and the lesson began.

The morning seemed to drag on for Joel and Jina. They were dying to talk to each other about their latest magical experience.

Finally the bell rang for first break. They both rushed out of their classrooms and met up under the big willow tree at the bottom of the playground. Joel normally played football during break, but today he just wanted to sit under the willow tree and speak to Judd – and maybe Francesca! Just then all of their friends came bursting through the long strands of the willow branches and sat down next to them, chatting away and eating their sandwiches. It was unusual for Joel and Jina's friends to be together as the boys were always teasing the girls.

This time was no different – after being there for only two minutes, the boys and girls started bickering with each other. The boys wanted to play football and they wanted Joel to come with them. But he only wanted to sit under the tree and talk to Francesca.

Then Keilash said, "Geez Joel, how did you think up that story this morning?"

"Keilash, you've got to believe me … it really happened, ask Jina."

Keilash didn't talk to Jina often, and if he did it was only to tease her. "No ways that story is true – it's impossible for all that to happen before school," he said.

"Anyway who cares? Come on Joel, let's go play foot ball! We're playing Sea Bay Junior on Monday and we have to beat them this time. Why are you sitting with the girls anyway? Do you like one of Jina's friends?"

With that, the boys started teasing him. "Joel's got a girlfriend, Joel's got a girlfriend!!!"

Joel got quite angry because he wasn't used to being teased. He also wanted his friends to understand the incredible lesson Magic had shared that morning.

He said, "Keilash, the story I told you in class this morning was true, and I'll show you. You go and play football and you want to score a goal, all you have to do is think about it and you *will* score one."

Keilash and his friends ran off to play football leaving Joel feeling bad about their little fight. But he knew he was right and went to go watch the game. He felt sure that what he had told Keilash about scoring a goal was true. But it didn't happen. Keilash never scored a goal.

He came up to Joel after the game and said, "See Joel, what are you talking about? I thought about scoring and I never did!"

Joel didn't know what to say. He was sure he knew how to use his **magical thinking**. Feeling dejected, Joel walked back to class, alone. The rest of the day dragged on; now not only was he fighting with his friend, but he also looked like a fool.

Finally the bell rang for the end of school. Joel found Jina at the bottom gate waiting for him. She could see that Joel was feeling down and they walked home in silence. As they entered the park, Jina felt it would be good if they sat by the river – somehow she knew it would make Joel feel better.

Joel asked Jina, "Why didn't it work when I explained to Keilash about scoring the goal? And why don't our friends know about **magical thinking** and **talking**? Everybody thinks I'm making this up, and now they're all laughing at me."

Because Joel had learnt how to use his magic, and his friends had not, he felt a little different to them. This bothered him because he really loved his friends, and he was a little afraid that they would not like him anymore.

Joel lay back, stared at the clouds and closed his eyes and, as it had done that morning, everything went very quiet.

The frogs stopped croaking.

The birds stopped tweeting.

The dogs stopped barking.

The stream carried on flowing over the boulders, but made no sound.

The rustle of the breeze through the trees stopped …

They both looked down to the end of the river, expecting to see the black hole appear in the reeds, but nothing happened.

They sat there for a while and then they heard that friendly voice.

"Hi guys!" said Magic, all bright and breezy.

They looked down at the river in front of them and there was Magic hovering just above the water.

"Wow!" he said. "You guys have had a really interesting day today, haven't you?"

Their answer was written all over their faces. Jina was smiling brightly and Joel was a cloud of concern.

Magic said, "Joel, your sister knows how to use her **magical thinking** and **talking** slightly better than you do.

This is because she spent more time on it this morning. You tried to explain to Keilash how to use his **magical thinking** and you were *almost* right. You told him to think about scoring the goal, but that is not enough. For us to achieve our goals, we must want it with all our hearts, we must believe that we can get it and we must practise. That's the part that you didn't tell him, and that's why he almost scored a goal, but missed.

"But you experienced something new, which Jina did not. What you learned today is that it's alright to be different from your friends. Your friends will come to understand you and like you just the way you are.

"You're very lucky because you have come to understand about your magic now, when you are only 11. Some people only get to understand it when they are really old – like 25 years old, and other people when they are even older! You must never think that you're better than Keilash or anybody else because you know about **magical thinking** and **talking** and he doesn't yet. But don't worry, you and Keilash will be friends tomorrow just as you were this morning.

"Now you go and have loads of fun," and with that he was gone.

Joel and Jina sat at the edge of the river for a while. Joel felt much happier as he thought about Magic's words.

After a while they got up and made their way home for lunch.

FUN TIME!

At times we think we are quite different from our friends and family. Write down five things that you think make you different from the rest of your family.

HAVE LOADS OF FUN!

9

The next morning Jina woke up earlier than expected. It was Saturday, and usually she would sleep in a bit, but today was the big day, the day of the gymkhana, and she was too excited to stay in bed. She jumped out of bed, brushed her teeth and got dressed. Instead of going down to breakfast, she sat on the edge of her bed and practised everything that Magic had told her.

She closed her eyes, did the relaxing exercise and imagined that she was sitting comfortably on top of Dreamchaser. She imagined him listening to her every command. Jina saw herself sailing over each jump and clearing the water jump by over a metre. As she visualised this, she repeated to herself what a good rider she was and how confident she felt. Using her **magical thinking** she saw herself going through the finish line after a perfect round, clearing all the jumps faster than

all the other riders. And she saw herself screaming with joy when the judges chose her as one of the new members of the national showjumping team. After a while she opened her eyes and went down to breakfast, her body tingling with excitement.

When Joel, Jina and her parents arrived at the gymkhana, a soft drizzle was falling from the overcast sky. Jina walked to the stables to fetch Dreamchaser and even though she had butterflies in her stomach, she wasn't as nervous as she thought she would be.

The judges read out the order in which the riders would jump – Jina was the final competitor. She was pleased because then she would know what time she would have to beat.

Jina was friends with two of the four girls that were also competing. They stood together talking about the other two girls that they didn't know and wondered how good they were. After a while she left them to go talk to her parents. Her father put his arm around her and said, "Jina, your mother and I know how badly you want to get chosen for the national team. But whatever happens today we just want you to know that we love you very much and that we are so proud of you. Just go out there and do your best!"

Jina hugged her Mom and Dad and told them she just needed to be by herself for a while before her ride.

She went into the stables and found a quiet place to sit and go over everything Magic had told her. Once again, she imagined everything as she had that morning in her bedroom and she repeated all the positive affirmations. When she had finished she walked out of the stables with Dreamchaser, feeling calm and confident.

As she eased herself into the saddle, Jina felt instantly connected to the horse. She felt like Dreamchaser knew what she was thinking and would react to her commands instinctively.

Jina glanced up at the scoreboard to check the times of the previous riders:

Contestant 1: Time 1 min 48 sec – **1 fault**
Contestant 2: Time 1 min 56 sec – **No faults**
Contestant 3: Time 1 min 54 sec – **No faults**
Contestant 4: Time 1 min 49 sec – **No faults**

Jina knew that she had to finish the course in a time of 1 minute 48 seconds or less, with no faults.

As she sat on Dreamchaser, she closed her eyes and imagined what the scoreboard would look like when she was finished jumping.

Contestant 1: Time 1 min 48 sec – **1 fault**
Contestant 2: Time 1 min 56 sec – **No faults**
Contestant 3: Time 1 min 54 sec – **No faults**
Contestant 4: Time 1 min 49 sec – **No faults**
Contestant 5: Time 1 min 45 sec – **No faults – WINNER!**

As Jina made her way into the arena, she was as focused as could be. When the starter's bell rang she was off like a shot.

The first jump loomed quickly before her. Everything was silent except for Dreamchaser's breathing and the slight squeaking of her saddle. She could smell the wet mud under her horse's feet and before she knew it she was sailing over the first jump, clearing it with inches to spare. She pulled tightly on the rein to turn right sharply. As she did so, she felt Dreamchaser's hooves sliding in the mud. She pulled hard on the reins just in time and the horse righted itself and lurched forward, eager to get to the next jump. But Dreamchaser was still slightly off balance as they both took off, and as he went over the jump his rear hooves hit the top bar. Jina's heart almost stopped! But as she landed, she looked over her shoulder to see the bar rattling around and safely settling back into position. With a loud "whoop!" she dug her heels into the sides of the horse. Dreamchaser went a step faster as they approached the dreaded water jump. Jina melted into the saddle, feeling connected to Dreamchaser like never before. In perfect slow motion, they went up over the jump together, Dreamchaser's back hooves clearing the water by over a metre. Now Jina knew that they were home safe. The last two jumps passed by in a flash and before she knew it, it was all over and she was slowly walking her horse out of the main arena.

As she was climbing off her horse she looked up to see the latest standings on the scoreboard.

Contestant 1: Time 1 min 48 sec – **1 fault**
Contestant 2: Time 1 min 56 sec – **No faults**
Contestant 3: Time 1 min 54 sec – **No faults**
Contestant 4: Time 1 min 49 sec – **No faults**
Contestant 5: Time 1 min 45 sec – **No faults –
WINNER!**

Joel and her parents came running towards her, showering her with hugs, kisses and happy congratulations.

Then one of the judges stood up and with microphone in hand and said, "Ladies and gentlemen, it gives me great pleasure to announce the names of the last two members of the national showjumping team. And they are Anisha Dasari and Jina …"

Jina found herself in a sea of well-wishers, ecstatic that her dream had come true. She was so overwhelmed with excitement that she didn't know whether to laugh or to cry. After a while, she slipped out of the crowd and went back to the stables where she sat quietly, running through all that had happened since she had met Magic the day before. She was so grateful that she knew about her magic and wished that Imagi-Nashun could be with her now. As she was getting up to leave, a small white feather came floating down and landed in her upturned helmet. Just then she knew that Magic was with her – and always would be.

On the way home Jina told Joel everything she had done to calm her nerves and to help her believe in herself. This time Joel *really* listened. When he got home he phoned Keilash and told him to come to the park and to bring a football.

FUN TIME!

Sit in a group or by yourself. Talk about and write down 5 – 10 things that you are grateful for in your life.

HAVE LOADS OF FUN!

10

Joel and Keilash played in the under-12 team, Joel in the midfield and Keilash as a striker. Keilash was very good and was the team's top goal-scorer, but sometimes he lost concentration and wasn't able to score.

On Monday afternoon they were playing their arch-rivals Sea Bay Junior. Every time the two teams clashed, it was an exciting, close game because they were so evenly-matched. The last time Sea Bay Junior had won 3–2 in a real thriller. This time Joel and Keilash wanted victory really badly.

Joel was sitting by the river when Keilash arrived. At first there was an awkward silence, both remembering their argument from the day before. But then Joel started telling Keilash about Jina's success that morning and began to explain all that Magic had told him. He told Keilash about **magical thinking**, explaining that he must think about and *see* what he wanted to achieve and while doing this, feel as if it was really happening. He described **magical talking** – how important it was to believe in himself and believe that he could do anything he put his mind to. Finally, Joel told Keilash that most importantly, he must have fun.

"And now we must practise football!" said Joel.

The friends spent the whole afternoon playing football together. They took turns shooting at the goal, dribbling against each other and practised passing the ball. By the end of the day their little argument was just a distant memory.

Keilash was so energised by their afternoon, when he went home he practised all Joel had told him. He sat on his bed and he imagined himself scoring a goal from a corner. And he imagined all his teammates running up to him and hugging him. He imagined the spectators clapping and cheering and he imagined them winning the game 2–0. He imagined how good it felt to score a goal and to be the hero of the team. He repeated to himself what a good footballer he was, and that he was a talented player. He lay down on his bed tingling all over and feeling happy that he and Joel were friends once again. When he finally fell asleep he dreamt about the upcoming game.

On Monday, the day of the game, Joel and Keilash arrived in the changing room thirty minutes before their teammates, and sat in silence. Both were feeling quietly confident that today, they were going to win. As the other players filed into the change-rooms, talking and shouting nervously, they sat quietly by themselves. Joel wanted to explain to his teammates about their **magical thinking**, but instead he just closed his eyes and thought of his own game.

He knew that Keilash was thinking exactly what he was and that they would have a good mutual understanding on the field. They had practised together Saturday, and all of Sunday, only breaking for lunch.

Their coach came into the changing room and said, "Guys, today has turned out to be a biggie. Riverside Primary lost on Saturday. That means that if we win today we will be the top team in the league. If Sea Bay Junior draw or win today then they finish on top. So let's go out there and do our best, and finish in first place!

All the players sat in dumb silence. Joel looked around and saw the nervousness creeping into his teammates. He knew he had to say something before they went onto the field.

"Listen up guys," he said. We're just as good as Sea Bay and there's no reason for us to be scared of them. We all want to win so let's just remember everything we've practised and play our hearts out. Don't be distracted by your parents, friends and the girls watching. Just focus on the game and have fun!"

Suddenly the change-room was alive with excitement. All the boys started whooping and cheering, their nervousness slipping away. The coach looked at Joel proudly and smiled.

FUN TIME!

Sitting in a group or by yourself talk about and write down 5-10 steps that you could put into practice to help you reach your goal.

Example:

If you want to run the 100-metre sprint for your school's athletics team then the list of steps to reach your goal could look like this:

Practise sprint training 3 times a week: Monday, Wednesday and Friday afternoons.

•   3x100-metre sprints, 2x 200-metre sprints and 2x 400-metre sprints.

•   Eat healthily so that I can have the right amount of nutrition and energy.

•   Do stretching exercises for 15 minutes every day before I get dressed for school.

•   Make a checklist to monitor how fast I am running my sprints.

HAVE LOADS OF FUN!

11

Ten minutes into the game all was not going well for Joel and his teammates. The left back slipped and miskicked the ball while passing to the keeper. The opposition striker pounced and scored. 1–0 to Sea Bay Junior.

Joel and Keilash watched their teammates' heads drop with disappointment. Everybody was shocked to be behind so early into the game. But the friends kept their cool. "It's not over yet, buddy! They got lucky and scored a goal. It's only the first half, we've still got lots of time."

The game went backwards and forwards, as the teams were evenly matched. The half-time whistle went and while they stood around eating their oranges the coach said to the team, "Guys, as Joel said earlier, we don't need to be scared of Sea Bay. They scored a lucky goal! We are good enough as a team and still have enough

time to beat them. In twenty minutes it will all be over. Have fun, play your best, and you'll be winners!"

The second half began just as the first half had ended, both teams evenly matched and neither able to get the upper hand.

And then ... Keilash intercepted a pass from the opposition and began charging towards the goal. He dribbled past the midfielder and was gaining ground when he realised he was on his own. His intercept had happened so quickly that none of his teammates were able to keep up! He dribbled past two more players and realised that now he only had the goalkeeper to beat. He focused on the top right-hand corner of the goal and kicked the ball as hard as he could. Because he had been running so fast, Keilash miskicked the ball slightly. Even though he had kicked it hard, it went just to the right of the goalie. The goalkeeper dived and just managed to get his fingertips to the ball, knocking it behind for a corner.

Joel now had to take the corner. Just as he was walking to the corner flag, Keilash came running up to him and said, "Joel. Just like we practised over the weekend. Just imagine that we're still in the park practising corner kicks."

Joel nodded and placed the ball next to the flag. He looked up to see where Keilash was standing. He was exactly in the spot where they had planned. For a moment he imagined that it was just him and Keilash practising football in the park across the road from his house.

Joel took a deep breath, ran three steps and kicked the ball as he had done so many times on the weekend. He watched as it sailed through the air towards Keilash. Just as he thought it was too late, Keilash jumped up higher than the defender in front of him and headed the ball into the bottom of the net. His teammates went crazy with happiness.

The spectators whooped with joy and clapped loudly. Joel ran over and gave Keilash a high five. The friends just smiled at each other.

The final whistle blew for the end of the game. The match was a draw, which meant that Sea Bay had finished at the top of the league. Even though they had both had fun and tried their hardest while playing the game, they were upset with the result.

FUN TIME!

Tear an A4 piece of paper into four equal pieces. Use lots of different colours to draw four different pictures of how you will look and feel when you achieve your goal. Stick the pictures onto your board.

HAVE LOADS OF FUN!

12

Joel and Keilash showered, got changed and started making their way home in silence. As they reached the bottom gate that led to the park, Jina and Francesca came running up to them. Jina said, "Joel, Keilash that was a fantastic goal, well done, you must be so happy!"

"We didn't finish top of the league because we didn't beat Sea Bay," said Keilash. "We believed we could do it and we never gave up, but we only scored that one goal."

Joel stood there not saying much, still thinking of the game. Even being so close to Francesca couldn't lift his spirits. He was lost in his own thoughts when Francesca asked, "Joel, I was wondering if you would come with me to Anisha's party on Friday night?"

Joel snapped back to reality with happy surprise. "Uh, s-s-su-sure," he replied, "I'd really like that!"

Jina just laughed. Although she never let on to her brother, she had always known that he liked Francesca.

"Come on Frannie, let's go to the library and leave these two to mope about the game," she said.

Joel and Keilash carried on their way, but now Joel couldn't stop smiling. The result of the game didn't sting as much anymore.

As they were crossing the river at the bottom of the park everything around them began to change.

The frogs stopped croaking.

The birds stopped tweeting.

The dogs stopped barking.

The stream carried on flowing over the boulders, but made no sound.

The breeze stopped rustling through the trees, and everything around them became much brighter.

Keilash looked at Joel with a very worried look on his face and stammered, "Wha-what's happening?"

Joel replied smiling, "You remember the story I told you about the oasis last Friday?"

Keilash nodded.

"Well, sit back and enjoy what's about to happen."

"Hello guys!" came a voice from above them.

Both of them spun around and looked up into the tree.

There on a branch sat Magic, this time dressed in their school football kit, boots and all.

Joel smiled.

"Hi Magic, good to see you again, nice choice of football kit."

Magic replied, "After watching your game today how could I not wear it? I am so proud of both of you."

Keilash was staring at Magic in disbelief.

"Hi Keilash, I'm Magic. Joel told you about me on Friday."

Keilash stared back, shock written all over his face.

"Now that you've seen I'm real, I'm sure you will believe all the stories Joel will tell you when he's late for school. I just wanted to meet you and to tell you both how well you've done."

Joel said, "But Magic, we practised and we used our **magical talking** and we saw ourselves winning with our **magical thinking** but still we didn't finish top of the league. How can that be?"

Magic replied, "Hey guys, I know it didn't go to plan. I know you really wanted to score that second goal to take you to the top of the league. It's not because you didn't do everything the way I told you to. It's just that sometimes it just goes like that. For us to get what we really want, it can take a little more time and effort than we expect.

"Just think – maybe Sea Bay also know about **magical thinking** and **talking** and maybe they practised just as much or even more than you guys did.

"The thing to remember is not to give up! If you really want something then a little challenge like today's result isn't going to put you off from trying again. But tell me, did you have fun today?"

"Yes!" they both replied.

"And you're friends again aren't you?"

"Of course we are!"

"And how do you feel about not winning the league?"

Just as Joel was about to answer Keilash said, "I feel a bit sad, but I know I tried my best. I had lots of fun over the weekend and today playing with my friends, and I want to try harder to take the league next year."

Magic smiled and said, "The more you use your **magical thinking** and **talking** the more positive thoughts you'll have, and the more fun you'll have. And now I must be gone. I will definitely be seeing you again shortly – and you too Keilash. Good bye!"

"Before you go there's just one more thing Magic," said Keilash, finding his voice. "Joel's got a girlfriend … Joel's got a girlfriend!" he shouted as he ran into the distance.

Joel threw his kit bag at Keilash and started chasing him through the park. Magic laughed out loud as he slowly faded away.

Joel caught up with Keilash, slapping him on the back he said, "Come on buddy! Let's go eat!"

FUN TIME!

Find a group of friends. Lie on your backs with your heads resting on another person's stomach forming a chain.

Laugh as loudly as you can for as long as you can. Wait and see what happens.

HAVE LOADS OF FUN!

www.ingramcontent.com/pod-product-compliance
Lightning Source LLC
Chambersburg PA
CBHW060040040426
42331CB00032B/1875